# American Archaeology

# UNCOVERS THE EARLIEST ENGLISH COLONIES

## LOIS MINER HUEY

**Marshall Cavendish**
Benchmark
New York

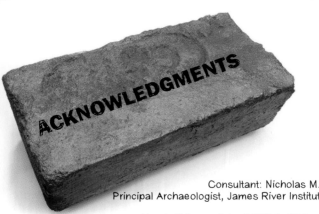

**ACKNOWLEDGMENTS**

Consultant: Nicholas M. Luccketti, M.A., RPA
Principal Archaeologist, James River Institute for Archaeology, Inc., Williamsburg, VA.

Marshall Cavendish • 99 White Plains Road • Tarrytown, New York 10591
www.marshallcavendish.us

Library of Congress Cataloging–in–Publication Data
Huey, Lois Miner.  American archaeology uncovers the earliest English colonies / by Lois Miner Huey.
p. cm.— (American archaeology)  Includes bibliographical references and index.
ISBN 978-0-7614-4264-6 (alk. paper)
1.  Virginia—Antiquities—Juvenile literature. 2.  Jamestown (Va.)—Antiquities—Juvenile literature.
3.  Roanoke Colony—Juvenile literature. 4.  Popham Colony—Juvenile literature.
5.  Great Britain—Colonies—America—History—Juvenile literature. 6.  Roanoke Island (N.C.)—
History—16th century—Juvenile literature. 7.  Fort Saint George (Phippsburg, Me.)—
Juvenile literature. 8.  America—Discovery and exploration—English—Juvenile literature.
9.  Archaeology and history—United States—Juvenile literature. 10.  Excavations (Archaeology)
United States—Juvenile literature. I. Title.
F229.H865 2010
973.2—dc22
2008050259

Photo research by: Tracey Engel

Front cover: *top*: Students conduct a dig at a university's science camp. Artifacts at bottom: *left*, a ceramic dish
fragment: *center*, a tobacco pipe; *right*, a collar plate from a suit of armor (all found at Jamestown).
Cover photo: AP Images/Bob Child (top); AP Images/Richmond Times–Dispatch, Dean Hoffmeyer (bottom, left); Getty
Images/Ira Block/National Geographic Images (bottom, center); AP Images/The Daily Press, Adrin Snider (bottom,
right); iStock © Lisa Thorinberg, iStock © Vishnu Mulakala, back cover; iStock © Alex Nikado
Title page: iStock © Lisa Thorinberg, iStock © Vishnu Mulakala

The photographs in this book are used by permission and through the courtesy of: *Alamy:* The London Art Archive, 12–
13; David Caton, 48. *AP Images:* Bob Child, 4; The Times Record, Terry Taylor, 28, 34; The Daily Press, Dave Bowman,
39 (bottom), 50; Richmond Times–Dispatch, Dean Hoffmeyer, 45; The Daily Press, Adrin Snider, 46; The Daily Press,
49 (bottom); The Daily Press, Joe Fudge, 54–55. *From the Collections of Maine Historical Society:* 27 (You can find this
image, item #7542, and thousands more at www.MaineMemory.net). *Corbis:* Bettmann, 9; J. L. Kraemer, Blue Lantern
Studio, 14; Lawson Wood, 40. *Getty Images:* J. Baylor Roberts/National Geographic Images, 18; Melanie Stetson
Freeman/The Christian Science Monitor, 22–23; Mario Tama, 32; MPI, 36–37, 43; TIMOTHY A. CLARY/AFP, 41; Ira
Block/National Geographic Images, 47. *The Granger Collection:* 15 (bottom), 24, 25. *Michael Halminski.* 19. *iStockphoto:*
S. Greg Panosian, 10–11. *Printed with permission of the New York State Museum, Albany, NY, 12230:* 5 (bottom). 3;
iStock © Eric Isselee, iStock © Kals Tomats, 4; iStock © ObservePhoto, 5; Shutterstock © Najin, 6; iStock © Richard
Goerg, iStock © Richard Cano, 7; iStock © Alex Nikado, 10; Shutterstock © Biuliq, iStock © Emrah Oztas, iStock © Jens
Stolt, 15; iStock © Norman Chan, 32; iStock © Wojtek Kryczka, 49; iStock © Torsten Lorenz

Printed in Malaysia
135642

# CONTENTS

# WHAT IS Historical Archaeology?

Archaeologists dig into the ground to find food bones, building remains, and tools used by people in the past. Historical archaeologists are looking for clues about what happened in America after Europeans arrived.

A group of students at the "Kids Are Scientists, Too" camp conduct an archaeological investigation at the former site of an eighteenth–century home on the University of Connecticut campus at Storrs.

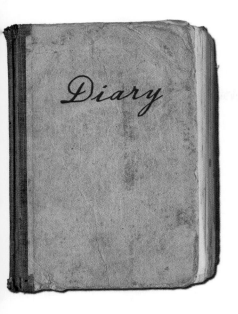

Yes, written documents tell some of the story. Historical archaeologists research documents like maps, diaries, land deeds, and letters to help understand what happened on a site. But those documents do not usually talk about regular people, the ones who did not write letters or diaries. Historical archaeologists are especially interested in learning about the lives of servants, poor farmers, and soldiers who built America.

How do archaeologists do this? By studying people's garbage.

What folks used and threw away tells more about their daily lives than objects kept on shelves out of harm's way. Archaeologists want to study the stuff that did not make it into museums—objects that were broken and discarded after much use. The garbage.

Broken dishes and glassware tell archaeologists what people of the past chose for setting their tables. Studying the bones of people's food, as well as their butchering techniques, provides information about what people ate and how they cooked. When archaeologists measure uncovered house and barn foundations, they find out how people crafted buildings, what size and shape they were, and how they were used. Buttons, straight pins, gun parts, and toys are clues to how people dressed, defended their homes, and spent their leisure time.

How do historical archaeologists know they are collecting information about people who lived in the 1600s rather than people from the 1800s? They use a method called stratigraphy (struh-TIG-ra-fee). Over time, layers of soil called strata build up on a site through natural causes or when people add their own materials. By carefully scraping away the soil with small tools, archaeologists dig down through time. They begin with upper levels of soil, in which they may find nineteenth-century layers. As they work their way down, they reach eighteenth-century layers, seventeenth-century layers, and so on. In some areas, the layers go back as far as Viking times. Prehistoric Native American layers are often found at the deepest level. The scientists dig each layer separately and collect its artifacts. Once the uppermost layer has been removed, the archaeologists have dug through the lives of everyone who lived on that site at a given time.

Based on what they find, archaeologists interpret the artifacts from each time period to understand how people's lives changed. *Change* is a big word in archaeology. How people lived—and how and when that changed— is an important part of the interpretation. As new evidence appears, archaeologists sometimes have to change their interpretations. That makes archaeology really interesting.

Stratigraphy is the key to understanding the past. Sticking a shovel straight down into the ground and pulling up the soil would disturb the stratigraphy, mix up the layers, and mix up the time periods. Archaeologists use shovel testing only to find a site. Then they switch over to small tools and painstakingly remove the layers one by one.

As archaeologists study a site, they carefully draw, map, and photograph building remains. Artifacts are taken back to the lab, where workers wash and store them. Codes are written on each object so that it is clear exactly where the artifact was found. Scientists run tests on charcoal, soil, and remains found inside bottles. Then the archaeologist writes up the results of the research so everyone can know what was learned. Museum displays often follow.

The world which we think of as ours was thought by people in the past to be theirs. Our knowledge of everyday events in the lives of people who lived long ago seems to be washed away by time. By digging in the ground and studying documents, an archaeologist seems to take a voyage to the distant past in a time machine.

Read about archaeology in books and magazines, go to museums, watch programs on television, and maybe visit a local archaeology dig. Someday you, too, might decide to use the tools of archaeology to study the past.

# The Earliest English Colonies

By the 1480s, European countries were competing to find a water route to the riches of Asia. This competition led to Columbus's famous trips westward. England entered the race late. The British hired an Italian named Giovanni Caboto (John Cabot in English) to sail west in 1497. Cabot rediscovered the rich cod-fishing grounds of Newfoundland that English, French, and Basque fishermen had visited for years.

John Cabot and his son, Sebastian, leave for America from Bristol, England. A replica of their ship, the *Matthew*, can be visited in Bonavista, Newfoundland.

During the reign of Queen Elizabeth I (1558–1603), English ships captured Spanish vessels loaded with riches from South and Central America. Men like John Hawkins and his cousin, Francis Drake, sailed the Atlantic Ocean and the Caribbean Sea. Along the way, they explored the land and raided Spanish settlements. Drake eventually sailed around the world and returned in 1580 to great acclaim. His trip established once and for all that England was in the game, too.

Drake's Bay

While sailing around the world, Francis Drake sought a place to anchor where he could repair his ships and gather food before taking off across the Pacific. He settled on a "faire and good Baye." His two ships landed on the coast of California in June 1559. This was the first-known English camp in what would become the United States.

In the 1950s a group of scholars decided to find the site. They concluded it was near today's San Francisco. But which of five nearby bays contained the site? Gradually all were eliminated except the one now called Drake's Bay. Here, archaeologists found artifacts from the 1500s, including six hundred fragments of Chinese porcelain from chests Drake had captured from Spanish colonies along the way and which he left behind. Other artifacts included ship spikes, water jugs, a Japanese cup, and some copper. Experts concluded that very soon after Drake left to sail across the Pacific, winter storms destroyed his fort and camp. Only artifacts were left behind to identify its location.

Drake's Bay, California. Archaeologists have found clues pinpointing this as the place where Drake and his crews stayed for thirty–six days in 1559.

MEOC

# One
# The Lost Colony
# 1585–1590

With the queen's blessing, two adventurous half brothers, Sir Walter Raleigh and Sir Humphrey Gilbert, outfitted 108 men for a voyage. They left for the New World in April 1585. Arriving off the coast of present-day North Carolina in June, they built a fort and houses on an island they called by its local Indian name, Roanoke.

This 1585 engraving shows the location of Roanoke, although the drawing of the actual settlement is not accurate, according to archaeological finds.

Sir Francis Drake on ship deck. Drake stopped at the Roanoke Colony.

This first group had been ordered to look for copper mines—not because copper itself was thought valuable, but because copper is found near silver. It was in the process of finding such mines that the first settlers had angered the local Native Americans, who actually valued copper even more than gold! The settlers had made such enemies of the Native peoples that, when Francis Drake arrived for a visit the following spring, the settlers decided to return to England with him. The men returned to England with maps and reports, including Thomas Harriot's studies of the Native Americans, the landscape, and the animal and plant life, as well as artist John White's numerous drawings.

A new group of 117 British settlers, including women and children, arrived at Roanoke in July 1587. They found the fort pulled down but the houses still standing, although overgrown with vines.

John White, the artist with the previous group of settlers, was now governor. Instead of continuing north to Chesapeake Bay, as planned, the new settlers stayed at Roanoke. They reused the houses and built new ones, perhaps including a fort. The colonists also worked to establish better relations with local Native Americans, but they succeeded only in befriending the Croatoan tribe.

In August, the colonists chose Governor White to return to England for fresh

Thomas Harriot returned from Roanoke and wrote a book about his experiences: *A Brief and True Report of the New Found Land of Virginia*, published in 1588. In the book, he described the local Native Americans and discussed minerals and rocks. Later, Harriot worked on mathematics, the study of eyes, and astronomy. He was the first to discover sun spots. He died on July 2, 1621. In Britain in 2009, the International Year of Astronomy focused on Harriot's work and Galileo's first use of the telescope for astronomical observations.

In Roanoke, John White drew what are now famous drawings and watercolors of the Native Americans, plants, and animals he saw. Little is known of White's life after his efforts to find the "Lost Colony." He lived for a while in Plymouth, England, and in Ireland, where he apparently mapped Sir Walter Raleigh's estates. His prints and drawings are housed in the British Museum.

## Thomas Harriot and John White

A llagatto. This being but one moneth old was 3. foote 4. ynches in length, and lyur in water.

*American Alligator* as painted in watercolor about 1585 by John White. Alligators are found in America and in China, so this image would have startled Europeans.

supplies. White left behind his married daughter, Eleanor Dare, and his grand-daughter, Virginia Dare, who had been born shortly after their arrival. Virginia Dare is celebrated today as the first English child born in North America.

War broke out between England and Spain. The frantic governor was unable to return to the colony until 1590, three years later. He was just a passenger on a vessel that spent most of its time raiding Spanish treasure ships in the Caribbean. Imagine his anguish as he waited, not knowing what had happened to the people he had left—his own daughter, son-in-law, and grandchild included! White finally reached Roanoke Island on his granddaughter's third birthday, August 18, 1590.

To his horror, everyone was gone. Climbing a bank toward the settlement, he and his companions saw the letters *CRO* carved on a tree. At the settlement area they found that the settlers had surrounded themselves with a palisade of thick tree trunks. The fence still stood, but the houses were torn down. One palisade post near the gate had the word *CROATOAN* carved on it. This stood for the name of the nearby, supposedly friendly, Native American tribe.

White and the settlers previously had agreed that they would carve a Maltese cross on a post as a signal that the colonists left in distress. But there was no cross. Did the colonists leave willingly? The houses were overgrown; iron and other heavy objects were strewn around inside the fence. The settlers had been gone quite a while. Their boats also were gone.

Where did the colonists go? Were they captured? White thought not. Because they had not carved the distress signal on the tree, he believed they were living with the Croatoan. White and the ship crew decided to go to where the Croatoan lived.

But his bad luck continued. A storm prevented White from landing at the Croatoan village. The ship crew decided to go to the Caribbean for fresh water and supplies and then return to the Croatoan village. Again, they were blown off course, all the way to the Azore Islands off Portugal. They gave up and returned to England.

White did not have enough money to finance another trip. Sir Walter Raleigh recklessly spent all his money and ended up in jail until the capture of more Spanish treasure ships made him wealthy again. In 1602 he sent out another expedition to find the Lost Colony. The men traded with Native Americans along the coast, but they felt it was too unsafe to look for the early settlers. Raleigh gave up.

To this day, no one knows what happened. Most people still call Roanoke the Lost Colony.

## Gone without a Trace?

By 1895, Roanoke, now called the birthplace of the American people, had been purchased for preservation. A monument to Virginia Dare had been erected, and the first archaeological digs

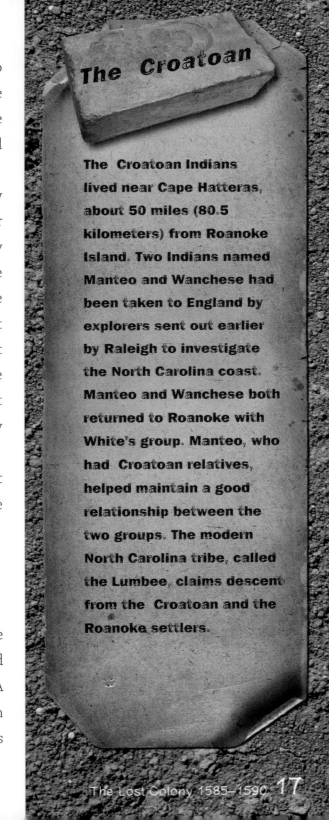

### The Croatoan

The Croatoan Indians lived near Cape Hatteras, about 50 miles (80.5 kilometers) from Roanoke Island. Two Indians named Manteo and Wanchese had been taken to England by explorers sent out earlier by Raleigh to investigate the North Carolina coast. Manteo and Wanchese both returned to Roanoke with White's group. Manteo, who had Croatoan relatives, helped maintain a good relationship between the two groups. The modern North Carolina tribe, called the Lumbee, claims descent from the Croatoan and the Roanoke settlers.

had been carried out. In the 1930s the fort was rebuilt with a log blockhouse, cabins, and a chapel along with an open-air theater for reenactments of the Lost Colony story. Later, the buildings were torn down, partly because they were falling apart but mostly because new research showed that the early English settlers did not build log houses.

In 1921 a movie company dug a long trench into the Roanoke fort while filming a story about the Lost Colony. All this construction work gradually destroyed parts of what seemed to be the original settlement. Extensive archaeology in the late 1940s uncovered an earthen fort. It was reconstructed in the 1950s, and it remains today.

# An Archaeology Mystery

Both before and after the archaeological work of the 1940s, scientists assumed that the earthen fort marked the site of both the first group of settlers and that of the Lost Colony. More work in the 1990s and later, however, has resulted in a new mystery. This is a perfect example of how new excavations produce evidence that leads archaeologists to change their ideas.

Excavations during the 1990s occurred just outside and inside the reconstructed 1950s earthen fort. The artifacts found were associated more with a laboratory than a house! The archaeologists had discovered evidence for a metallurgy shop—a place where rock was melted down to extract metals. Lumps of copper waste showed that copper was being analyzed at the site. Excavators found more evidence of scientific work: the presence of glassware used in both chemical and distilling processes. They also found Indian pottery; crucible pots encrusted with melted copper; and coal, flint, iron scaling, and a lot of charcoal.

An archaeologist works at the Lost Colony site. He is using a dust pan to sort through the excavated soils for artifacts he may have missed.

These were very important finds—evidence of the first such industry in the United States!

But a metallurgy shop, with its hot fires and fumes, would not be built inside or near a fort or houses. This meant the earthwork that had been found and reconstructed was not the site of a fort. Instead, the earthwork probably sheltered the metallurgist and his helpers who were part of the first group of settlers.

## Tools and Trade Beads

During excavations of the earthwork in the 1940s, excavators found an iron sickle lying in the moat—a protective ditch dug around the earthwork. This sharp-edged tool probably was used to cut weeds and grass before building the earthen fort. They also found a carpenter's auger, with its screw tip and pieces of T-shaped handle, that settlers used to make holes in wood; in fact, some wood still clung to the auger's tip. Old iron spikes were mostly found all together, as if left in a pile, or inside a container that since had vanished. Other iron fragments were an iron bar and a possible hinge fragment.

Reminders of the trade with the local Native Americans included a glass trade bead and three brass disks with one or two holes in each one. The disks were no doubt offered as necklaces in exchange for food or other goods. In Europe, workmen moved these disks around a table to keep track of goods. All three of the disks found at the site had been manufactured by a company in Germany between 1550 and 1574. The disks are very thin with a design on each side. Disks like these appear in other sites from the 1600s.

Another brass object found in the earthwork ditch was part of a balance weight used to weigh objects, probably metals or even medicines. One of the two musket balls found had been fired. At the earthwork? By accident? No one knows.

Despite excavations in areas away from the earthen fort, the houses have not been located. Where were they?

Some researchers now suggest that the settlement was closer to water. At low tide below a cliff that is eroding into the ocean, a National Park historian found a barrel and a hollow log. Radiocarbon tests on the wood indicated that the barrel was used in the 1500s. If this is the bottom of an old well shaft as researchers supposed, the Lost Colony's fort and village site may have been located there. More work may uncover evidence of occupations—if it has not all eroded into the sea.

## America's Baffling Loss

The Roanoke Colony remains lost. The houses and fort have not been found. We still do not know where the second group of settlers went after they left their home.

Meanwhile, archaeologists are excavating Croatoan sites to study the Indians themselves while they look for some evidence of Europeans living there. So far, although some artifacts from the 1500s have been found, there is no definite proof that the lost colonists went to live with the Croatoan.

# Two
# The Popham Colony, 1607

Remember Sir Walter Raleigh and his half brother Humphrey Gilbert of the Roanoke Colony? Gilbert tried again to establish a colony in what we now call Maine. However, his ship wrecked, and he drowned in 1593. His son, Raleigh Gilbert, kept trying.

Site of the Popham Colony on Sabino Head, Maine. After excavations, the site was filled in with clean soil to protect the archaeological remains.

In the early years of the 1600s, other Englishmen tried to settle, too. But none succeeded.

Finally, in 1607, a private group called the Virginia Company decided to establish two colonies. One was to be in Maine (the Popham Colony), the other in Virginia (Jamestown). The Popham Colony was named for Sir John Popham, Lord Chief Justice of England and the man who put the most money into the venture. The second was named for King James I, who had succeeded Elizabeth I to the throne.

In May 1607, two ships carrying more than one hundred men left a British port and sailed for the coast of Maine. Led by Captain George Popham, nephew of the chief sponsor, and Captain Raleigh Gilbert, the group included army officers, soldiers, a gunner, a blacksmith, carpenters, farmers, and a man assigned to search for mines. Arriving on the Maine coast in August, the men took small boats up today's Kennebunk River and chose a place for the colony. Construction began on August 20.

A nineteenth-century wood engraving shows the artist's interpretation of Native Americans greeting the Popham Colony settlers in 1607.

According to the records, "all the companies Landed and thear began to fortefye [fortify]. . . . Captain Popham Sett eh [the] fryst sytt [site] of ground . . . and the rest followed & Laborded hard in the trenches." For days, "all hands Laborded hard about the fort."

While the walls of what they named Fort St. George were going up, some carpenters began building a small sailing ship for the colonists' use. They named the ship the *Virginia*.

When the fort walls were completed, the settlers started a storehouse inside. When this was almost finished, the ships were unloaded and prepared to return to England. Realizing they would run out of food over the winter, the colony leaders sent fifty men and boys back to England on the ships. That left forty-five colonists.

To set up the fur trade, Raleigh Gilbert explored up and down the Maine coast before winter and met with various Indian chiefs. Native Americans later complained that the English beat them and set their dogs on them. Gilbert obviously did not do well dealing with the Native Americans.

A nineteenth-century wood engraving shows the artist's interpretation of the Popham colonists setting their dogs on Native Americans.

Captain George Popham died that winter, and twenty-five-year-old Raleigh Gilbert was left in charge. The colony was resupplied in the spring and again in the fall of 1608, but by then, the colonists had decided to go home. Raleigh Gilbert's older brother had unexpectedly died in England, so Raleigh had inherited land and a title. With their captain dead and their young leader leaving, the colonists were unwilling to face another cold winter. They had found no rich mines, relations with the Indians were poor, and the fur trade had been unsuccessful.

Settlers at Jamestown, after much struggle, succeeded in establishing the first permanent English settlement in America. The Popham colonists, on the other hand, gave up—and the site of their fort mostly was lost. Between 1608 and 1994, the fact that Englishmen had tried to start a colony in Maine was largely forgotten.

# Finding Fort St. George

When the first ships returned to England from Maine in 1607, one carried a drawing of Fort St. George. This was the only detailed plan of any English settlement in North America. The draftsman had drawn the fort as completed, but not enough time had passed for twenty-five structures to have been built inside. Much later, one of the goals of the archaeological work was to find what actually was built.

Over the years, many changes had taken place at the site where the archaeologists thought the fort was located. Deep plowing had disturbed historic layers, and the U.S. Army had built a modern fort called Fort Baldwin in 1905. A railroad had been constructed, piers had been added on the waterfront, and extra buildings had been built outside Fort Baldwin— fortunately mostly without foundations or cellars. However, deep utility

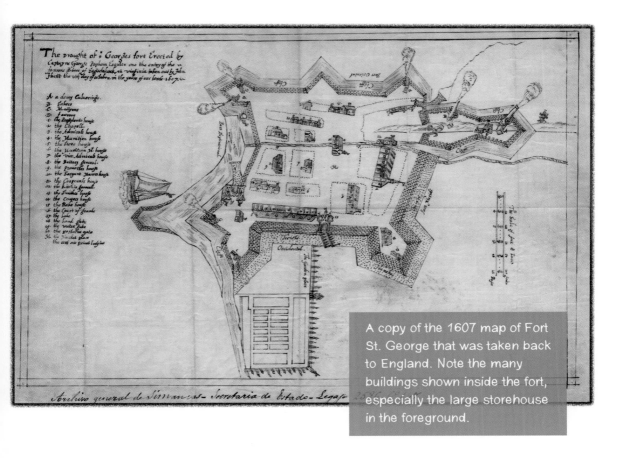

A copy of the 1607 map of Fort St. George that was taken back to England. Note the many buildings shown inside the fort, especially the large storehouse in the foreground.

trenches, postholes, and other modern intrusions had been added. Also, other excavators had attempted to find the old fort and then left their trenches and excavation holes behind.

The U.S. Army gave Fort Baldwin to the State of Maine to use as a public park. Research on the location of old Fort St. George, as well as the overlay of the 1607 drawing on modern maps, indicated that some of the fort was located in the park. The rest of it lay under private land bordering the park.

The archaeologists worked long and hard to deal with all the disturbances and to find what remained of Fort St. George. Once they located the main storehouse, they were able to find other structures, the market space, and the fort walls.

# The Storehouse Story

The storehouse was the best-built structure of Fort St. George. It was framed with timber and supported by large posts in the ground. The walls were filled with wattle and daub (a mixture of clay and sticks) for insulation, and the floor was packed earth. Excavators knew it had a thatched roof, because charred thatch was found on the floor and around the outside walls.

The storehouse was 10 feet (3 meters) shorter and somewhat wider than what was shown on the map. Military artifacts were concentrated in one corner, while glass trade beads and iron washers were in the middle. This suggests how items were grouped on shelves—useful material, like trade beads and construction hardware, was kept close to the door. The small size and scatter of the artifacts indicates that larger items were removed before the storehouse was destroyed.

Archaeologists excavate Raleigh Gilbert's house site at Fort St. George. The bucket of soil in the foreground will be sent through a screen to check for artifacts the excavators might have missed.

# Hearth and Home

The house of President Popham has not been found, but archaeologists did discover the house of Raleigh Gilbert. And it was not much of a house.

Gilbert's dwelling was crudely constructed by putting two forked tree limbs together into the ground and laying other timbers across them to make a roof. The walls were made of clay and straw mixed with water. The roof was made of sticky clay over wood and was covered with thatch.

Inside, there was a stone hearth built of stones held together with more clay. Judging by the many pieces of hard black daub, the hearth was surrounded by a wattle-and-daub smoke hood and a chimney built on posts.

A heavy concentration of melted window glass, burned metal artifacts, and postholes in the center of the house indicated that there had been a fire while someone lived in the house. The burned part had been hurriedly rebuilt. Some burned posts had been replaced by new ones. Old ones were filled with fire debris. A second, unburned layer of artifacts had accumulated both inside and outside the house. This meant someone lived in it after the fire and then abandoned it for good.

Although this was not a fancy house, it did contain the only glass window found on the site. Raleigh Gilbert had brought a glass window with him and, even though this house was no mansion, he had installed it anyway. His ownership of the only window in the colony showed that he was a leader.

The house also contained many musket balls, lead dropped while casting them, and lead scrap from trimming them. Most of the ammunition Gilbert made was for a pistol. He must have owned a type of expensive, highly decorated small gun that gentlemen of the period carried. Although he did not leave the pistol behind, the artifacts on the floor of his house showed that he had such a gun. Excavators also found a fragment of a dagger blade and pieces of armor that Gilbert once wore.

Most of the decorated dishes found at the St. George site came from Gilbert's house. Blue and white eating vessels were scattered around the hearth. Others were medicine jars. There were many fragments of glass bottles that once stored liquors. Delicate wine glasses were present, also. It seems as if Gilbert tried to live somewhat as he had at home. He also still dressed like a gentleman; over fifty fancy black buttons were found in his house—apparently he kept losing them! Trade beads that had been dropped on the floor and lost showed that the young commander was carrying on his own private trade with local Native Americans.

Raleigh Gilbert not only lived in a not-very-fancy house here in the wilderness, but his house (and maybe others in the fort) had burned, probably during the winter. It had been rebuilt hastily. Perhaps after this experience and loss of many of his belongings, Gilbert was only too happy to return to what he now owned in England: a manor house, land, and a title!

Several buildings shown on the 1607 map are not mentioned in any documents. Thus, finding those buildings would be a true test of how accurate the map was. Among the missing structures was a building used to store liquor, a guardhouse for soldiers assigned to keep settlers from stealing the liquor, and more houses.

As it turned out, archaeologists found the liquor storage warehouse and its attached guardhouse near the main storehouse. The provost's house for the sheriff of the colony and a jail, however, apparently never were built, nor was a house for the munitions master (guardian of weapons). Artifacts identified one dwelling with large numbers of musket balls and lead scraps as the possible munitions master's house, located in a different place than shown on the map.

# A Fake "Lake"?

Labeled on the 1607 map was "the lake." One of the objectives of the excavations was to find this feature. By doing documentary research, the archaeologists discovered that in the 1600s, the word *lake* referred to a small stream or a channel deliberately cut for water—a definition different from today's. Archaeologists found that the "lake" indeed was an artificial channel cut by the settlers. The channel diverted water so that it flowed through the fort for their use. The settlers were engineers, too!

The map showed small unlabeled dwellings across the lake. These were probably homes for less important settlers. Postholes of the type found elsewhere on the site were uncovered, but they did not line up enough to indicate walls. The buildings probably were of the same type as that built for Raleigh Gilbert, with forked posts that supported the roof. Modern disturbances in this area had destroyed much of the evidence. However, artifacts like wattle and daub, iron nails, ceramics, and glass suggested these were house sites.

Excavating the area shown on the map as "The Market place" showed that it definitely was an open area containing no buildings. Few artifacts were found. Its very emptiness, however, supports the idea that it was an open space set aside for trading, drilling of soldiers, and meetings.

# No Boats in This Moat!

The archaeologists were surprised to find a very shallow ditch that they realized was the moat around the fort walls. The 1607 workers had used soil dug from the moat to form the fort walls. When they hit a layer of thickly packed cobbles, they widened their digging to get the soil they needed. The moat turned out to be 20 feet (6 m) wide. Because it was so wide, it did not need to be deep, too!

# Ground-Penetrating Radar

Ground-penetrating radar is a non-digging method of "seeing" underground. A machine shoots radio waves downward as it gets dragged over the ground's surface. The waves bounce off underground objects and features while a printer in a nearby truck prints out lines on a chart. Archaeologists use this method to find such hidden features as hearths and burial shafts. Excavations then concentrate on those areas.

These archaeologists are using a ground–penetrating radar (GPR device to conduct a survey of a vanished nineteenth–century village in New York City's Central Park.

Archaeologists brought in ground-penetrating radar to help them search for more of the moat. The machine showed that the moat extended on all sides of the fort, so the archaeologists did not need to uncover it all to find out how large it was.

After ten years of work on this difficult site, the archaeologists concluded that much of the 1607 map was correct. When the map was drawn, some of the structures had not yet been built, so the map shows some buildings that had only been planned. But the major structures were in place. The lack of stone foundations, the small number of people living there for only about a year, and the heavy reuse of the property in the centuries that followed made finding traces of this fort very difficult. But the archaeologists outlined the fort, discovered that dwellings were built on posts set in the ground, and established which ones were not built.

Evidence of these first homes is important for understanding the experience of settlers in the New World. The men came with certain ideas about what a house should look like, but in this wilderness, even the leader learned to settle for a hut, cottage, or hovel—at first. Raleigh Gilbert's house was much less well built than the storehouse, but at least it contained a glass window. The other houses were simple huts, perhaps not much more than wigwams, an idea borrowed from local Native Americans.

# What Do the Artifacts Tell Us?

The supplies that settlers brought to the colony were some of the least expensive available for that time period. Apparently these supplies were considered good enough for a new colony. The ceramics were mostly low-quality wares from West England, but they also included Spanish and German storage jars and jugs, as well as Dutch pots. The military remains were pieces of body armor, gun parts, and lead shot.

A view of excavations at Fort St. George from outside a shelter. The tepee-like structure supports a screen through which excavated soils are placed and examined to be sure no artifacts were missed. Note the mounds of soil already screened!

Almost every house had the same goods in terms of ceramics, glass, and military items, although the leaders' dwellings had more of each. Colonial leaders' belongings included fine wine glasses, a mirror, fancy buttons, and even a small gold ball that apparently was a decoration on some object. Evidence showed that it was Raleigh Gilbert's house that had burned, not the main storehouse as documents suggested. The quick repair of his house and the types of artifacts found there reveal that Gilbert enjoyed a higher status than others.

# Failed, but Not Forgotten

The Popham Colony was a well-planned settlement. The men pulled together to build a solid fort in about a month, created a fine ship, and made an accurate map. The excavations of the site showed that the planning and organization of the colony was much better than previously had been thought. These men found themselves in a New World, but they adapted and did their best to establish a "new England." The Popham Colony failed—but future settlers learned from their mistakes.

# Three
# Jamestown: The First Successful English Colony

The Jamestown settlers left England a few months before the Popham Colony setters, and arrived on the coast of Virginia in May 1607. They chose an island for their fort. The small island contained marshy land and bad drinking water. However, the colonists had their reasons for locating there. First, they had instructions to choose an island, if possible, for safety. Second, the fort would be situated up a river with a safe harbor. Third, local Native Americans had already cleared the land. Finally, there were no Indians living there in 1607.

A modern image of the 1607 landing of English settlers at Jamestown

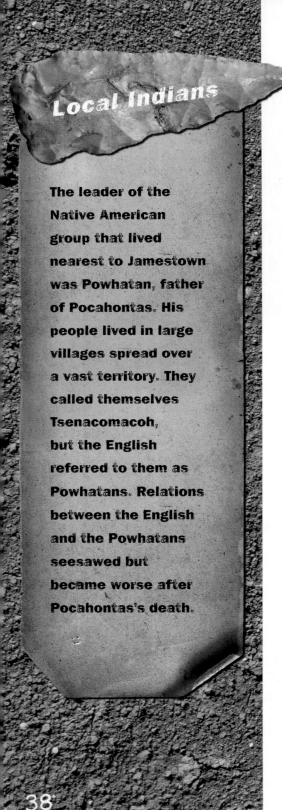

## Local Indians

The leader of the Native American group that lived nearest to Jamestown was Powhatan, father of Pocahontas. His people lived in large villages spread over a vast territory. They called themselves Tsenacomacoh, but the English referred to them as Powhatans. Relations between the English and the Powhatans seesawed but became worse after Pocahontas's death.

The poor water supply and unhealthy air from the swamps were not as important as protection. People in the 1600s did not drink much water, but they did dig a well to get water for tasks like laundry. Meanwhile, the river water probably looked clear in May, when they arrived, and did not turn murky until later. The swamps had high, rich land for growing crops. The Jamestown settlers built their fort on the island's highest ground.

The settlement grew in fits and starts. Many problems developed among the colonists and with the local Powhatan Indians, despite John Smith and Pocahontas's famous friendship. During the winter of 1609–1610, known as "the starving time," crops failed and the settlers died in great numbers. Survivors decided to leave. They set off down the James River toward the ocean. On the way, they met an advance ship announcing the arrival from England of a new governor, more settlers, and, best of all, food! Governor Thomas West, Baron De La Warr, persuaded them to turn around and try again. After that, Jamestown succeeded.

According to one source, by 1624, seventeen years after the Jamestown colonists

The first settlers did dig a well, which John Smith pronounced had "excellent sweet water." The archaeologists found another well, which had been built later, full of artifacts. Tests on the water in this well showed that, despite the number of years that had passed and the amount of chemicals in the soils today, the water still was clean enough for drinking! When it was in use, various objects had been dropped into it, either on purpose or by accident. Then, when the well was abandoned sometime in the 1620s, the shaft was filled with even more material.

In all, more than 1,400 objects were found. These included drinking vessels, tools, a child's shoe, clay pipes, and bricks used to line the well's sides. Most surprising were scattered pieces of what amounted to a full suit of armor. The pieces came from a helmet, front and rear pieces to protect the wearer's neck, a breastplate, and several front hip and thigh plates. It seems the Virginia heat persuaded the owners to rid themselves of this hot metal in favor of lighter forms of protection.

## Exciting Discovery: Jamestown Well

Visitors to Jamestown watch the excavation of a seventeenth-century well, one of two dozen found at the site.

# The Sea Venture

In 1608, one of the supply ships sent to Jamestown, the *Sea Venture*, wrecked on the island of Bermuda. On board was John Rolfe, who later married Pocahontas. The 150 passengers lived on shore while they built two new ships. They set sail for Jamestown in spring 1610. There they found only sixty colonists out of 215 still alive after "the starving time." The turtle oil, smoked hog and fish, and barrels of flour and meal they had rescued from the *Sea Venture* wreck probably extended the lives of the desperate Jamestown settlers long enough for Governor De La Warr and supply ships to arrive.

In 1958, divers found the remains of the *Sea Venture* buried in sand off the Bermuda coast. They brought up its wooden bottom, cannon, and other artifacts, which are now on display at the Maritime Museum nearby. Many people think that when the story of the *Sea Venture* was told in England, author William Shakespeare used it to write his famous play, *The Tempest*.

A reproduction of the *Deliverance*, built by the *Sea Venture* crew and sailed to Jamestown. It can be visited on St. George's Island, Bermuda.

arrived, they numbered 1,232, with twenty-nine different settlements scattered along the James River. Some of the people elected men who met to represent them in 1619. This was the beginning of representative government in America. Jamestown remained an important port—and the capital of Virginia—until the 1690s, when the state government moved to Williamsburg. Today, Jamestown is an important historic site visited by thousands who want to learn more about the brave Englishmen who were first to settle successfully in the New World.

Over the past four hundred years, scientists came to believe that the site of the Jamestown fort had eroded into the river. One archaeologist who thought otherwise persuaded the owners of the land, the APVA Preservation Virginia, to let him look for the fort. By himself, he started excavating in April 1994. Almost immediately, he found artifacts from the early 1600s. By summer, a crew joined him, and they still dig at the site today. They have uncovered almost the entire outline of the fort, which is shaped like a triangle with bulging corners. Building remains, over a million artifacts, and skeletons of early settlers have been excavated and studied.

Today, stockade posts outline the original fort location, and a new museum displays artifacts and skeletons alongside interpretations of life in early Jamestown. Queen Elizabeth II traveled to America in 2007 to help celebrate the anniversary of this first successful English colony in North America.

Queen Elizabeth II of England inspects soil being screened for artifacts during a tour of Jamestown in 2007.

# Three Sides, Three Weeks

When the Jamestown settlers arrived, the men made a fort of tree trunks and brush. Attacks by Native Americans in late May made it clear that this structure was not enough.

A new, triangular fort was completed in three weeks. Archaeologists estimated that the colonists cut and trimmed six hundred trees, dug a trench 1,000 feet (305 m) long and over 2 feet (.5 m) deep, and upended enough posts to make a stockade wall 11 to 15 feet (3.5 to 4.5 m) high. Builders secured the posts by packing thick clay around their bases.

According to historical documents, the builders produced enough flat boards to fill three ships returning to England. To accomplish all this, everyone present must have worked. Despite the stories about the behavior of "gentlemen" at Jamestown, this was not a lazy bunch of men lying around doing nothing—at least not while they feared for their lives!

# Life inside the Fort

Archaeological evidence revealed that at first, settlers lived in cellars dug inside the fort, probably roofed over by leaning wood and thatch. Four of the uncovered cellars never developed into buildings. The completed cellars were one room wide and many rooms long.

Colonists constructed barracks by driving forked tree limbs into the ground and framing them with wood, just as the settlers did in the Popham Colony. The walls were made of thick earth covered with saplings and thatch. The cellar under the east end yielded coins dating from 1590 to 1602; disk counters made in Germany like those found at the Lost Colony; lead tokens; lead seals used to seal cloth bundles; window glass; and body armor—all evidence of life in the barracks after 1607.

Settlers in Jamestown traded trinkets and copper to the region's Powhatan Indians in exchange for meat and corn.

Because of the threat of Native American attacks, settlers stayed inside the fort during Jamestown's "starving time." In the cellars there was evidence of strange kinds of food: poisonous snakes, butchered horses, dogs, rats, and cats. These help confirm the stories of how desperate the settlers were during the winter when so many starved to death. An X-ray of one dog's skull showed an embedded bullet that had healed over. The dog was a large mastiff; greyhounds also were present. These dogs were used to hunt food. The Native Americans recognized the dogs' importance to the English, so they frequently fired weapons at the dogs. The mastiff had survived an Indian attack, but not the starving time. The fact that they killed their precious dogs for food showed how desperately hungry the settlers were.

In the largest of the mud-walled buildings, a wood-lined cellar was located under the southernmost room. Excavators found stains from two wooden

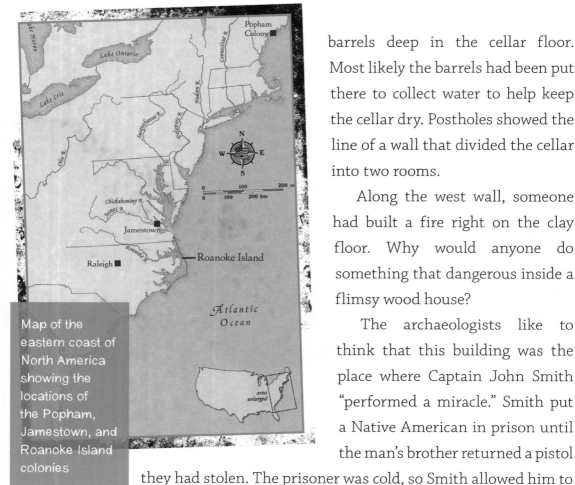

Map of the eastern coast of North America showing the locations of the Popham, Jamestown, and Roanoke Island colonies

barrels deep in the cellar floor. Most likely the barrels had been put there to collect water to help keep the cellar dry. Postholes showed the line of a wall that divided the cellar into two rooms.

Along the west wall, someone had built a fire right on the clay floor. Why would anyone do something that dangerous inside a flimsy wood house?

The archaeologists like to think that this building was the place where Captain John Smith "performed a miracle." Smith put a Native American in prison until the man's brother returned a pistol they had stolen. The prisoner was cold, so Smith allowed him to build a small fire. The fire had no flue, so the prisoner fainted from lack of oxygen. When the brother returned, he thought the prisoner was dead. But Smith gave the fainting man some alcohol and brought him "back to life." Both were so impressed with Smith's powers that they returned the pistol and went to tell others. Smith claimed he had few problems with the Native Americans after that.

All of these buildings were similar to ones the settlers knew in England. Later on, the colonists learned better building techniques from the Native people. They used bark for walls and roofs to keep out the hot Virginia sun.

## What Do the Artifacts Tell about the Jamestown Colonists?

Archaeologists uncovered many Native American artifacts in the fort, including more than two hundred points for arrows and spears, many pots, reed mats, and evidence of making shell beads. Contrary to what was previously thought, Indians were frequent visitors to Jamestown. Historians think that many Native women married colonists, cooked, and did laundry for the settlers. The two groups enjoyed a more personal interaction than is evident in the records. The settlers welcomed their many Indian friends and trading partners and treated them as guests.

In the first group of settlers, there were twenty men assigned to the task of farming. Since Native Americans had already cleared the land, the colonists

Artifacts excavated at Jamestown. The upper objects are early ceramics that would have been part of eating equipment used in the fort. At the bottom is a cannon ball (left), and part of a rapier, a type of sword (right), shown before treatment in the lab.

planted seeds right away. But the crops failed and famine followed: twenty-five men died in August and September of the first year.

Also in the first group were forty men assigned to search for gold and other precious metals, in hopes of finding wealth like the Spanish had in South America. Jamestown excavators found instruments used to weigh metals, along with tools needed to pull gold out of stones in which it was found. The searchers did not find gold, diamonds, or rubies, but they did find amethysts, garnets, and quartz crystals. The investors in England were disappointed.

Some workers also made brass. The local Native Americans considered copper and brass very valuable. More than eight thousand strips and shavings of copper were found in the early layers at the Jamestown site.

A collar plate from a suit of armor, found at the Jamestown excavations in 1988

The soldiers sent to guard Jamestown Colony quickly found that their body armor was not practical in Virginia's hot weather. Archaeologists found that many parts of such armor had been thrown away. One breastplate had been made into a crude metal bucket. Meanwhile, the soldiers marched, drilled, had target practice, and watched for enemies.

Artifacts showed that the settlers were busy and industrious people. Tools such as axes, hatchets, and gouges showed that the carpenters cut down trees and sawed boards in a saw pit discovered outside the fort. The blacksmith worked, too, as evidenced by a horseshoe found in an early layer and by the large amounts of slag, waste iron, and thousands of handmade nails. Brick hearths found inside the fort's buildings were the work of brick makers and bricklayers. Also present were tools used for barrel making, including a plane, drill, broad axe, and adze. Colonists had pins, needles, thimbles, and buttons to make and mend clothes. Smoking pipes made of local clay were common, so someone had set up a business of making clay pipes with the same decoration as that on pipes made in

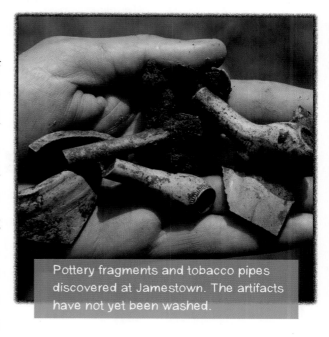

Pottery fragments and tobacco pipes discovered at Jamestown. The artifacts have not yet been washed.

England. Evidence of glassmaking included pots holding melted sand and glass waste, thousands of window-glass pieces brought from England to melt down as part of glass manufacturing, and a cobble glass furnace. Eventually, however, the glassmakers decided they could do better smuggling weapons to the Indians. For their foolishness, all had been killed by Indians before 1609. Glassmaking did not resume until the 1620s.

The colonists adopted new foods. In the early layers, excavators found fourteen kinds of wild bird bones, as well as bones from eight different mammals, marine creatures, twenty-five kinds of fish, and reptiles. Colonists captured their prey with fish hooks, net weights, and line sinkers. Judging by the remains, about half the settlers' meat came from the wild. Did they hunt much more than historians originally believed? Or did the Native Americans bring in all this food to trade?

Records were kept by men who could read and write, judging by the presence of an ink well, pencils, wax seals, and signet rings used to stamp a person's identity into the wax.

Jamestown was a busy place, a town within and outside walls where crafts were practiced, crops raised, Native Americans both befriended and made into enemies, soldiers drilled, food cooked—and funerals held.

## Boning Up on Bones

A burial uncovered inside the fort walls. A gunshot wound to the lower leg caused this person's death.

Inside the fort, excavators discovered the grave of a twenty-year-old man. Most likely he was buried there so the Native Americans would not realize that colonists were dying. He lay in a wooden coffin and was wrapped in cloth pinned together with large straight pins, as was the custom. Although his teeth were bad, the scars left by muscle attachments on his bones showed he had been strong. He was 5 feet 9 inches (175 centimeters) tall. He had died from a gunshot wound. The angle of the shot showed that the shooter had been standing behind him.

The archaeologists guessed that the young man was participating in a military drill when he was shot by another musketeer. Such a drill consisted of the first line of men firing off their muskets, then marching to the side while the second line stepped forward to fire. Many accidents occurred during this maneuver, as guns went off by accident when the second line moved forward. What a commotion that must have caused! A lead musket ball and twenty-one smaller lead shot were found with the bones.

Tests on the man's bones showed that he died in 1607, so this incident happened within the first months of settlement. According to the records, a

# Bone Studies

Human bones provide a wealth of information about a person's life. Measurements of the skull and study of the teeth help determine the person's age, gender, and ancestry. The condition of bones from the spine, legs, and arms—including the marks that muscles leave on them—helps show what kind of work the person did. Scientists use the length of the leg bones to determine a person's height.

Finally, using tiny bone samples, scientists can obtain a radiocarbon date. Charcoal produced by burning bone (and wood) contains a trace amount of radioactivity left from when it was alive. This decreases through time at a regular, measurable rate. By counting the rate at which the radioactivity has decreased in the bone, a scientist can count back in time and arrive at the approximate date when the bone ceased to be alive—that is, the date of the person's death.

A person's face can be reconstructed from skull bones, sometimes with the aid of a computer to fill in missing parts. Although the results take some guesswork, the reconstructions are amazingly lifelike. The faces of both the young man and the woman buried inside the fort were reconstructed. They are on exhibit at the new Jamestown museum.

Reconstruction of the faces of a man and a woman who were Jamestown settlers young English gentleman, Jerome Alcock, died of a gunshot wound in August 1607; the modern theory is that he was shot by one of his own!

Found buried nearby was a white woman over the age of forty. Her cause of death was not established, but since the first women arrived in 1608, her death must have occurred after that. Her bones showed she had done much hard work during her life.

Buried outside the fort was Captain Bartholomew Gosnold, identified by parts of a captain's staff buried with him. He stood about 5 feet 3 inches (160 cm) tall, and tests showed he died in his mid-thirties. Records confirm that Gosnold died of illness at age thirty-six in August 1607. Gosnold was important—he was a sailor and explorer who in previous trips to the New World had named Cape Cod and Martha's Vineyard off the coast of

This skeleton is believed to be the remains of Captain Bartholomew Gosnold, a high–ranking colonist who was buried outside the fort.

New England. He helped plan the Jamestown expedition, raised money, recruited settlers, and voyaged with them to Virginia. Probably because he was so important that Native Americans would notice his absence, he was buried outside the fort with great fanfare—musket volleys, prayers, and singing. That early in the colony's history, this kind of ceremony displayed the settlers' strength and was meant to impress the watching Indians.

Altogether, twenty-one graves were found inside the fort. Some held more than one body. At least one—a young teenage boy—died from a Native American attack, judging by an arrow and a stone point found next to his leg. His shoulder bones also showed injuries. Four boys were present in the first group to settle at Jamestown, but it is impossible to determine which boy this was. Samuel Collier and Nathaniel Pecock may still have been alive after 1610, but no information about James Brunfield and Richard Mutton has been found. The boy probably was one of the latter two.

In the 1950s earlier archaeologists had discovered many graves in another area outside the fort. In addition to studying those bones, these archaeologists looked for more. They found sixty-three graves with skeletons from seventy-two different people. The earlier, deeper graves had been carefully dug, the bodies laid out in the usual manner. Later graves placed over the deeper ones, however, were dug in a hurry, and the bodies were not arranged as carefully. Pieces of clothing were found in these later graves. One man had a tobacco pipe and a spoon in his pocket. Since clothes were expensive and usually were passed on to other family members, these people probably died of disease. Their caretakers were in too much of a hurry to undress them and wind them in cloth. One woman had copper pins in her hair, showing that she was a lady, but she had been wedged into a shipping crate rather than a regular coffin—another indication of a hasty burial.

## Tree Ring Studies

Trees produce growth rings each year. By counting the rings, anyone can calculate the age of the tree. The width of each ring depends on how much rain the tree received in a given year. By comparing the widths of tree rings from many trees (a process called dendrochronology), the weather for each year can be determined. According to the surrounding trees, 1606–1613 were years of severe drought at Jamestown. This made food production very difficult.

Some of the people had died of wounds, but the occupants of these later graves no doubt were victims of the 1609–1610 starving time. Many died in their twenties (the men ranged in age from twelve to twenty-five; women ranged from twenty-six to thirty years). Fourteen percent of those buried were infants under the age of two.

Most surprising was part of a skull found in one of the fort's trenches. It belonged to a middle-aged man who had suffered a violent blow to the head, probably from a Native American's stone axe. Circular cuts indicated that surgeons tried to save him by drilling through the skull to relieve the pressure of brain swelling. However, the drill could not cut through the bone, and the man died. Saw marks on the skull showed that the surgeons conducted an autopsy to study why the man died! They removed the complete top of his head. This indeed was surprising. The practice of autopsies was entirely new information about medical care in the Jamestown fort. This discovery, along with the many medicine jars and medical instruments found by the archaeologists, meant that real attempts were made to save colonists' lives.

# Unsettled Settlers—Almost

Recent tree ring analysis indicated that there was a severe drought in the Jamestown area from 1606 to 1613, right after the colonists arrived. In addition to managing relations with Native Americans and suffering unusually cold winters, the colonists had to fight dry conditions for many years.

The settlers were not prepared for the hot Virginia climate. Their body armor wore them out, food spoiled easily, insects spread disease, and people fought with each other. Still, settlers kept coming—even women and children after 1607. Somehow, life at Jamestown seemed more promising than life at home. Despite great bouts of sickness and starvation, the colonists hung on. They adapted to the climate, the food, and the hard work. As a result, Jamestown became the first permanent English settlement in North America.

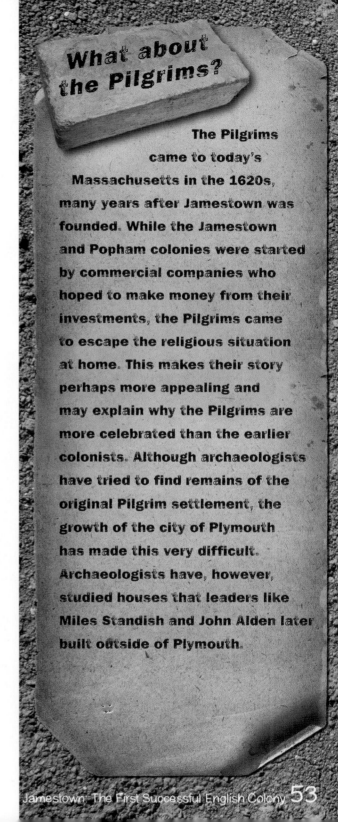

## What about the Pilgrims?

The Pilgrims came to today's Massachusetts in the 1620s, many years after Jamestown was founded. While the Jamestown and Popham colonies were started by commercial companies who hoped to make money from their investments, the Pilgrims came to escape the religious situation at home. This makes their story perhaps more appealing and may explain why the Pilgrims are more celebrated than the earlier colonists. Although archaeologists have tried to find remains of the original Pilgrim settlement, the growth of the city of Plymouth has made this very difficult. Archaeologists have, however, studied houses that leaders like Miles Standish and John Alden later built outside of Plymouth.

# Four

# What Archaeologists Found Out

Although the English got a late start in colonizing North America, they were eventually the most successful. After establishing Jamestown in 1607, they went on to colonize or take over other nations' territories until there were thirteen English colonies stretched along the eastern seaboard, with Canada to the north.

An archaeologist takes photos of a newly-uncovered sunken fireplace hearth and well inside the James Fort.

Archaeological excavations in the three earliest settlements—Roanoke, Popham, and Jamestown—show the faltering steps England took toward colonization. The British learned from their failures, however. For example, metal armor does not work well in a hot climate! Jamestown was a close call, but in the end, it was their first success.

Archaeologists have uncovered information about what kinds of shelters were built, what foods were eaten, and what goods were thought necessary for a successful colony. Archaeologists also have studied the layout of these settlements, analyzed the stresses on the colonists' lives as shown on their skeletal remains, and discovered the beginnings of the metal industry in the United States. This information about everyday living, seldom mentioned in documents, grabs our attention. The people and their struggles become more real, their lives more fascinating—and our admiration grows even stronger.

**1496** King Henry VII hires John Cabot and his son Sebastian to sail west.

**1497** The Cabots reach the east coast of North America.

**1559** Francis Drake and his crew camp on the coast of California for thirty-six days.

**1562** John Hawkins takes his first journey to New World.

**1567** John Hawkins, accompanied by Francis Drake, sails to the West Indies.

**1572** Francis Drake attacks Spanish harbors in America.

**1573** Francis Drake sees the Pacific Ocean for first time.

**1577–1580** Francis Drake makes an around-the-world voyage.

**1582** The first English colony in Newfoundland, Canada, is founded.

**1585** Sir Walter Raleigh and Sir Humphrey Gilbert send the first group of settlers to Roanoke.

**1587** The second group of settlers stays at Roanoke; Governor White returns to England.

**1588** The English defend themselves against Spanish invasion (the Spanish Armada).

**1590** Governor White returns to Roanoke and finds the settlers gone.

**1595** Sir Walter Raleigh explores the Orinoco River in South America.

**1602** Sir Walter Raleigh sends an expedition to look for the lost settlers.

**1607** Jamestown is founded.
Popham Colony is founded.

**1608** Popham colonists return home in the fall.
A supply ship for Jamestown, the *Sea Venture*, wrecks off Bermuda.

**1608–1609** Jamestown experiences a "starving time"; many colonists die.

**1610** The *Sea Venture* crew arrives from Bermuda in new boats; a new governor and supplies arrive.

**1614** Pocahontas marries John Rolfe, and they have a son.

**1617** Pocahontas dies in England; Rolfe and his son return to Virginia.

**1619** The first black slaves arrive in Jamestown.

**1620** Pilgrims come to Massachusetts aboard the *Mayflower*.

# GLOSSARY

**adze** —An axe-like tool with a curved blade for smoothing wood surfaces.

**auger** —A carpenter's tool with a screw tip and a T-shaped handle, used to drill holes in wood.

**Basque** —Describing a group of people from a small area of northern Spain.

**broad axe** —An axe with a broad blade used to cut and shape timber.

**captain's staff** —A long wooden pole, topped with a decorated metal point, that officers carried to lead their troops in marches and battle.

**cod** —A type of fish widely used in Europe.

**crucible** —A container that can resist high heat and is used to melt ores and metals.

**distilling** —A process of first heating and then cooling to separate different parts in a mixture; the results are more pure than the original materials.

**earthwork** —Piles of earth used to form structures.

**excavate** —To dig and uncover objects in the ground.

**flue** —An opening that allows gases and smoke to escape a building.

**gouges** —Chisels with hollow blades used to dig channels in wood.

**Maltese cross** —A cross whose arms look like arrowheads pointing inward; named for the island of Malta off Italy.

**metallurgy** —The act of melting ore to extract metals.

**Newfoundland** —An island off the east coast of Canada; frequently visited by Europeans during explorations of the New World.

**plane** —A tool used for smoothing the surfaces of wood.

**porcelain** —A type of china invented by the Chinese.

**slag** —Waste that gets separated from metals during various processes.

**thatch** —Straw, rushes, palm leaves, or other plant material used to create a roof.

**wattle and daub** —A mixture of clay and sticks put inside building walls for insulation or used to build chimneys.

# Books

Brain, Jeffrey. *Fort St. George: Archaeological Investigation of the 1607–1608 Popham Colony*. Augusta: The Maine State Museum Publications in Maine Archaeology, No. 12., 2007.

Cooper, Michael L. *Jamestown, 1607*. New York: Holiday House, 2007.

Fitz, Jean. *The Lost Colony of Roanoke*. New York: G. P. Putnam's Sons, 2004.

———. *Who's Saving What in Jamestown, Thomas Savage?* New York: G. P. Putnam's Sons, 2007.

Kelso, William M. *Jamestown: The Buried Truth*. Charlottesville: The University of Virginia Press, 2006.

Miller, Lee. *The Mystery of the Lost Colony*. New York: Scholastic, 2007.

# Websites

http://library.thinkquest.org/3826/intro.html

This site presents the mysterious Roanoke story, told by cyber space characters who were once the colonists there.

http://www.pophamcolony.org/

Learn about excavations at Fort. St. George, Raleigh Gilbert's house, and the storehouse. Also check out the list of Popham colonists, the "Gentlemen of Quality."

http://www.virtualjamestown.org

Visit this virtual village and find out how buildings at Jamestown looked.

# DVDs

The History Channel, DVD Disc 2: *Roanoke, the Lost Colony*. From Digging the Truth Series 2.

*Pocahontas Revealed. Jamestown (Va.)*. Boston: WGBH Boston Video, 2007.

FURTHER INFORMATION

# Books and Articles

Aker, Raymond and Edward Von Der Porten. *Discovering Portus Novae Albonis: Francis Drake's California Harbor.* Palo Alto, CA: Drake Navigators Guild, 1979. Report of the scholarly group set up to find Drake's camp.

Ames, Glenn J. *The Globe Encompassed: The Age of European Discovery, 1500–1700.* Upper Saddle River, NJ: Pearson Prentice Hall, 2008.

Brain, Jeffrey, with Peter Morrison and Pamela Crane. "Fort St. George: Archaeological Investigation of the 1607–1608 Popham Colony" in *Occasional Publications in Maine Archaeology,* No. 12, Arthur Spiess, ed. Augusta: The Maine State Museum, the Maine Historic Preservation Commission, and the Maine Archaeological Society, 2007.

"Popham: The First English Colony in New England" in *Avalon Chronicles: The English in America 1497–1696,* Vol. 8, pp. 87–116, 2003.

"The Popham Colony: An Historical and Archaeological Brief" in *The Maine Archaeological Society, Inc. Bulletin,* Vol. 43, No. 1, Spring 2003, pp. 1–28.

Harrington, Jean Carl. *Search for the Cittie of Raleigh, Archaeological Excavations at Fort Raleigh National Historic Site, North Carolina.* Archaeological Research Series, No. Six. Washington, D.C.: National Park Service, U.S. Department of the Interior, 1962. Account of the excavations of the late 1940s.

Kelso, William M. *Jamestown, The Buried Truth.* Charlottesville: University of Virginia Press, 2006. The basic source for the results of the ten years of work at Jamestown fort.

Kelso, William M., Nicolas M. Luccketti, Beverly A. Straube, Eric Deetz, and Seth W. Mallios. *Jamestown Rediscovery* I, II, IV, V, VI, VII. Richmond: The Association for the Preservation of Virginia Antiquities, 1995–2001. Booklets of between thirty and seventy-six pages analyzing the finds of that year's field season.

Lange, Karen E. *1607, A New Look at Jamestown.* Washington, D.C.: National Geographic, 2007.

Morrison, Jim. "In Search of the Lost Colony" in *American Archaeology*, Vol. 10, No. 4, Winter 2006–2007, pp. 38–44. Archaeology on Croatoan village site.

Noel Hume, Ivor. *The Virginia Adventure: Roanoke to James Towne, An Archaeological and Historical Odyssey.* New York: Alfred A. Knopf, 1994. The story of early English attempts to settle in North America by one of America's leading archaeologists.

"The Riddle of Roanoke" in *Avalon Chronicles: The English in America 1497–1696*, Vol. 8, pp. 57–86, 2003.

Potter, Charles W. III. *Fort Raleigh.* Washington, D.C.: National Park Service, U.S. Department of Interior, 1985.

Schulte, Brigid. "Dig Casts New Light on Indian Culture: VA. Archaeological Findings Unveil Complex Society." *Washington Post.* August 22, 2007. Article about excavations at the legendary Powhatan Indian site.

Skowronek, Russell K. and John W. Walker. "European Ceramics and the Elusive 'Cittie of Raleigh'" in *Historical Archaeology*, Vol. 27, No. 1, pp. 58–69, 1993. Reexamination of the ceramic finds at the site.

Von Der Porten, Edward P. "The Drake Puzzle Solved" in *Pacific Discovery*, Vol. 37, No. 3, July–September 1984, pp. 22–26. Study of the Chinese porcelain from the Drake Site. Succeeded in identifying those left there by Drake.

Page numbers in **boldface** are illustrations and charts.

## About the Author

Lois Miner Huey is a historical archaeologist working for the State of New York. She has published many articles about history and archaeology in kids' magazines as well as a book biography of the Mohawk Indian woman, Molly Brant. She and her archaeologist husband live near Albany, New York, in an old house with four affectionate cats.